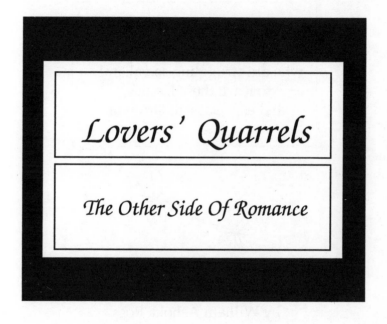

Lovers' Quarrels

The Other Side Of Romance

William Ashoka Ross
&
Judy Ford

To all the lovers of good heart
who are struggling so valiantly
to learn these lessons,
and especially to Uruvara.

Playful Wisdom Press
Judy Ford & Company
P.O. Box 834
Kirkland, WA 98083
For information, call   206/ 823-4421

$4.95 / ISBN 0-9619246-1-6

Lovers' Quarrels

The Other Side Of Romance

A QUIET WORD TO THE READER

Welcome to **Lovers' Quarrels!** We've collected 127 outstanding lovers' quarrels. *Why?* Because reading these lovers' quarrels is both fascinating and instructive. At a certain point you'll probably rub your eyes, amazed that people like you (*normal* people!) actually do these things. Maybe you'll slap your forehead and say, "*Hey!* What's going on??"

There is a conspiracy of silence about lovers' quarrels. Nobody really talks about them. The subject is a closely guarded secret — *almost as closely guarded as Pentagon secrets!* In a way, lovers' quarrels *are* military secrets. People are very tight-lipped about them. So just in case you thought you were the *only* one who got into squabbles, we have news for you: *you're not!*

We decided mostly to let these situations speak for themselves — to present what one reader has called *"the absolute nitty-gritty of human existence."* We chose to narrate these situations as brief scenarios written in "shooting script" style, unornamented, unadorned. Novels, plays, poetry and musicals have been written about some of these basic situations; they probably will be again. These are perennial dramas.

What can you learn from **Lovers' Quarrels?** *To avoid the pitfalls!* To recognize strategies of domination and techniques of manipulation, regardless of whether these are your own or someone else's — and regardless of whether they are deliberate or semi-conscious. To see the patterns leading to conflict and, hopefully, avoid those patterns the way you might avoid a torpedo or a booby-trap requires considerable skill. To open our heart and forgive is a lot easier provided we're willing to do it.

Lovers' quarrels are *not* small potatoes! A huge chunk of the billions of dollars and rubles, etc., that are spent on armaments every single year could be saved if the lovers' quarrels portrayed in this book were to be adequately resolved and dealt with.

Why do people fight? And what can be done about it? We have some ideas for you in our commentary. You may want to read it in bits and pieces, as you go along, or you may not want to read it until you've read all the fights in this book — or at least enough of them to have your own insights about what **Lovers' Quarrels** are all about. Some people read the entire commentary from beginning to end. *Whatever works best for you!*

One reason we quarrel is because we're so serious. We seem to relish agreement more than playfulness. *We want to be right!* And as long as we want to be right, we are playing with fire. That's why we call ourselves *Playful Wisdom Press*. Playfulness, to us, is a non-serious peek-a-boo with life.

We've enjoyed visiting with you, and if your love life improves, even ever so slightly, as a result of this book, we will feel tremendously rewarded!

"YOU NEVER"

He says, "You never want to make love."
She replies, "And you? You never help
around the house!"

YOU REALLY
HURT ME

Lovers' Quarrels
are the pitts...

"You really hurt me last night," she says.
"I did?" he asks. "How?" "You don't
have any idea of what I'm talking
about?" "No," he says, "I don't." Gayle
gives him a cold hard look and says,
"Well, if you're that insensitive, there's no
point in my telling you." Then she turns
her back and walks away.

From heaven you are suddenly cast into hell.

It is so unexpected, so shocking and upsetting,
such a jolt to the system!

EX-HUSBAND

He: "I don't want to be here when your ex-husband comes." She: "How shitty of you to leave just when I really need you!"

HONESTY PUNISHED

Betty finally talked to him honestly about her feelings. Which wasn't easy for her, and now she expects some appreciation. But instead, Ryan is mad because he disagreed with the feelings she expressed! She exclaims, "I thought you wanted me to tell you honestly how I felt, but every time I do, you just get mad at me." This last remark of hers really makes Ryan's blood boil, especially since he knows it's probably true. "Well," she asks, "do you want me to tell you what I'm feeling or don't you?" After a few more exchanges like this, the silence is like lead.

One moment everything is fine, the next moment your insides have crumbled. You feel like a fish

AFRAID OF SEX?

Somehow Roger invariably manages to start a fight whenever Liz gets amorous. The issue isn't important; the effect of the fight is to move them away from sex. After a while she realizes what's going on: "You're afraid of sex!" she says. "You pick fights just to avoid having to have sex!" All of which, of course, leads to a humungous fight.

HAIR

She: "Why do you leave whiskers all over the sink, Michael? And can't you __ever__ put the toilet seat down?" He: "Stop being such a perfectionist! Besides, I thought you said you loved me."

that's been yanked out of the water and thrown into the dirt. Your stomach feels as though it's inside out, your heart seems to have collapsed, and you're either flushed with anger or crying. Again and again you try

DOUBLE TAKE

Zelda asks: "Can we go out for a while and do something fun for a change?" Dan says "You bet, sure we can." Then five minutes later he says, "Oh, I forgot, there's some work I need to do." She feels confused, angry, worried. Letting Dan know she's upset might scare him off. She doesn't know what's going on or what to say.

"WHY DID YOU COME?"

She asks him to come visit her relatives. Ben doesn't want to. She says: "Come on, we'll have a good time." He finally agrees. On the way he starts getting depressed. While they're there he hardly says a word. Afterwards she's angry at him and says: "If you were going to be grumpy, why did you come along?"

to express what you're feeling, to talk sensibly about it, but one way or another, you keep on making a mess of it.

TOOTHPASTE

He : "Don't squeeze the toothpaste in the middle! And why don't you ever put the cap back when you're done?" She: "Why are you so picky?"

POETRY

She notices that Hugh lies about little things — where he had lunch, how much he paid for his new shirt, and so on. This puzzles Tricia, but when she tries to talk with him about it, he shrugs his shoulders. "You're too serious," he says. "There's no poetry in your soul and very little humor; if there were, you'd enjoy life more." "Look," she says, "I want us to be truthful with each other. Why must you be so evasive?"

Quarrels begin so unexpectedly. One moment all is sunshine and then, once again, you feel as though you've been hit in the stomach.

You know they call them lovers' quarrels, but they

LATE FOR DINNER

...*standing there over the stove, one eye on the cookbook and the other on the clock, newly married, trying to juggle things so everything will be ready at 6:30. Happy as a lark with what she's doing, looking forward to when Randy comes home from the office. The only thing is, an hour later she's still waiting for him, and feeling so let down she doesn't know what to do. And then, when it's almost 9:45 p.m., the door opens. Randy walks in, and he acts as if everything was perfectly natural. But seeing the mood she's in he asks, "What's wrong, honey?" And she feels so hurt, she can't bring herself to say a thing.*

just feel like sheer agony to you. You try and try to make the other person understand, and despite your best efforts,

COUNSELING

They go to a relationship counselor who tells them to use plenty of I-and-you language and to acknowledge their feelings. After a while, Ed says: "Every time I say anything that she doesn't want to hear, she says: 'That's not true.'" Molly, instantly: "That _definitely_ isn't true!"

TEASE

He: "You never admit to a single fault, do you?" She: "If I did, you'd never let me forget it." He: "You're really convinced you don't in any way contribute to our relationship difficulties." She: "That's not true." He: "And as long as you're convinced that it's all my fault, things will never improve between us." She (laughing): "Oh, I do have a fault — I like to tease you when you're being serious!"

you just don't succeed. What to do? The books all make it sound so easy — so you must be the biggest jerk of them all! You try to reason — you point out you've done everything just the way your lover wanted you to. You've tried and tried — and it isn't enough. You've goofed again. You feel like rushing out

WONDERFUL

She: "You're so wonderful, so sensitive, so sexy..." He: "Greta, I really need more time for myself." She: "I hate you, you son of a bitch, how can you do this to me??"

IN THE MOOD

Arlene is doing the dishes when Greg comes up behind her and puts his arms around her. She's just been feeling sorry for herself, complaining silently that he never, ever, offers to do the dishes. Feeling resentful as she does, she now goes all stiff when he embraces her. This confirms him in his belief that Arlene is basically frigid. Nothing is said and he goes to his study to read a magazine. Then for the next few weeks she wonders why he never wants to make love to her anymore.

and throwing yourself under a train or into the grinding wheels of some grotesque machinery. If only it were all over! You go absolutely berserk inside, "bananas," and there's no place to turn.

BIRTHDAY

Marilyn knows Jonathan never remembers her birthday. So this time she reminds him — two weeks ahead of time! He says something that sounds like "Uh-huh." Then she wonders: is he going to give her something? And what on earth will it be? When she finally unwraps the present, she can't believe her eyes. Lo and behold if it isn't a multi-colored mop with twelve interchangeable sponges! Marilyn smiles, grits her teeth and says, "Why thank you, Jonathan!" What she feels inside she can't possibly bring herself to say.

Is there anything to equal the torment you feel when the person you love, your sweetest friend, doesn't understand you? When she or he gives you a hard time? It's a torture beyond description, and, what's even worse,

YOGA

She has started meditating and doing yoga and bringing her weirdly dressed friends home for herb tea. "What kind of people are these, Margaret?" Ron asks, perturbed. "Very nice people," she answers, "who understand something about what life is really all about." He decides not to say anything but he's afraid she's going through a mid-life crisis and wonders if she'll end up joining a cult.

TAILOR-MADE

She finds out Lee is having an affair with a fashion model. And she knows it's not the first time. So with bitterness and glee she goes to the clothes closet and she cuts one arm and one leg off every one of his suits. Then she changes all the locks and places his clothes in a neat pile outside the front door. Having done this she calls a taxi and leaves for Florida. The next time they meet is in a lawyer's office.

you tend to feel you can't tell anyone about it. Why? Because on the one hand you don't want to say anything bad about about the person you love, and because on the other hand you're afraid of being

CRITICAL MAN

Whenever they go any place, Jason makes very critical remarks about everyone and everything. That woman is gross, the food in the restaurant is cold, so-and-so is a phony, etc. She tries to point out to him how critical and negative he is, but he won't see it and throws it back at her. "Well, you're criticizing me, aren't you? Aren't you the one who's being critical?" "I'm simply trying to point out to you what you do," she says, "and you don't want to hear the truth about yourself." "Boy," he says, "talk about the pot calling the kettle black!"

boring or being thought of as a complainer. So you're alone with your grief and your pain whatever you do.

Sometimes you decide that things have gone about as far as they can go. You *know* you're going to get a divorce. You know the relationship is over. But what happens?

ONE-UP

Norton likes to use complicated words. In their early days, Sylvia would sometimes ask him what a word meant but he always chortled and said, "You mean you don't _know_?" and soon she stopped. His favorite line is, "Where've you been all your life?" When she tries to talk to him, he interrupts her in 'helpful' ways — either saying, "Slow down, don't talk so fast, nobody can understand a word you're saying," or telling her "If you don't raise your voice and speak up, people are going to fall asleep." If Sylvia has some grievance, he'll say "Never mind about yesterday, yesterday is gone forever," or "Never mind about that, that isn't important." Or he'll take a word she's using and totally take it apart ("Commitment? Do you know what that really means?") Another of his favorite lines is, "When you get to be my age you'll understand." She would like to boil him in oil.

When you see the person who caused you all that anguish, suddenly everything is all right again. The love is immediately there again, and you receive a warm hug and a kiss (or give one). And suddenly,

AWFUL PERSON

Tessa asks Craig to come to a talk she's giving. Afterwards she insists he tell her exactly what he thought. "It was very good," he says. Tessa says, "I hear a 'but' in there somewhere. Please tell me what you really thought." "Well, I thought you spent too much time looking at your notes," Craig replies. "It would have been better if you would have related more to the audience." Tessa's response to this is: "So what you're really saying is that I gave an awful talk and made a fool of myself. Aren't you? I guess I'm just an awful person." This irritates him because he gave her the honest criticism she asked for. They don't actually fight but there's a heaviness that lingers.

you can't imagine what the fuss was all about. It's as though you've been smitten with amnesia. You can't exactly remember what you fought about, you feel all kinds of emotions, and you hardly know if you're coming or going. And you can't help wondering: what witchery is this?

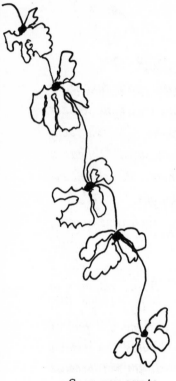

TRAVELING MAN

His job requires a lot of travel, so Eric is mostly home only on weekends. Every time he tries to involve himself with the kids, they get into a hassle. "That's not the way we do it when you're gone," they tell him, and she asks, "How can you expect the rules to change to suit you?" "You're treating me like an outsider," he protests resentfully. "Well, you are," Tracy says, "you're never here!" "That's not my idea," he points out, "but somebody's got to earn the money." "Then why," she asks, "don't you get a different job?" "You think it's that easy?" he says. "Anyway, if I were here every night, you'd nag me to death even worse than you do now!"

Soon you say to yourself: nothing on earth could be worth this much aggravation. You feel trapped, caught by some invisible flypaper. You don't seem to be able either to go forward or to go back. You don't know if your relationship is over, or almost, or if you're just going through a transition. Sometimes you get so weary with fighting,

RELAX

He: "We've got to take the videos back, Patricia, it's important to be on time."
She: "Les, you've got to learn to relax, you're too rigid!"

NUDITY

Nudity embarrasses Ruth. So she never undresses totally in his presence. Even when they're making love. This turns him on but at the same time annoys him because he thinks people should be undressed when they make love. What's more, he regards her embarrassment about being naked as a sign that she doesn't fully trust him — because why, otherwise, would she be putting such an unnecessary barrier between them? Nothing is ever said, but he does feel resentful. She can tell that something is wrong, but she can't for the life of her figure out what it is.

you don't ever want to get close to another human soul again. You can hardly believe there can be so many misunderstandings! And you wonder: why can't things ever go right? You want to go toward

THE PAST

Arnie coaxes, nags, and wheedles, insisting he wants her to tell him all about her previous relationships. Paula does. A day later, he says: "You slut, how can I ever trust you again?"

STEPCHILD

"I'd like you to develop a good personal relationship with my children." That, anyway, is what she says. But when Frank tries, the kids make fun of him. "You don't insist they're to respect me," he complains, "instead of being supportive, you're undermining me!" Helen hates his helplessness. "I guess you'll just have to work things out yourself," she shrugs. He feels he's being had and he seethes inside. Then one day he suddenly yells at her about something totally unrelated, and she can't understand why on earth he's so angry.

the person you love, and you're afraid you're going to run into a buzz saw — or into a brick wall! You feel as though you're being bulldozed, and you don't know what to do. Sometimes, you even wish

SECRETS

Chloe talks things over with her friends. Dwight talks to no one about anything personal. So of course he's shocked when he discovers she tells what he regards as family intimacies to strangers. "They're not strangers," she insists, "they're my best friends." "Well, I don't know them," Dwight says, "and anyone outside our family is a stranger as far as I'm concerned." "You don't know them because you don't want to know them," she answers. He says: "I think telling them some of the things you do is disloyal." She dismisses his objections by saying, "You're being ridiculous!"

you were dead! You hear single people talking about how they'd like to get married and you think to yourself, "Just wait till they find out!"

Sometimes it hurts so much, it's all you can do to drive your car to work...

EITHER / OR

Ralph was brought up with the idea that kids should be seen but not heard. Emily grew up in a family that gleefully made children the center of attention. He expects the kids to be quiet; she feels invigorated when the kids rush in and out. He insists the kids only watch TV on the old black-and-white set downstairs; she permits them almost everything. One day they're having dinner when he tells the kids to eat what's left on their plates. She says "They don't have to." He feels overruled and, of course, belittled. He goes into cold anger and says, "Emily, you _always_ interfere when I'm disciplining the kids." "I have to, Ralph," she says, "because you're too..." He interrupts her and says, in that hard silent way of his: "Either you're going to start disciplining the kids, or I'm moving out."

...and then, when you get to your office, everybody wants you to smile! And if you say anything to anyone, they tell you to "get over it," and then someone else gives you a pep-talk

DATING EXPENSES

They're going to the theater and then out to dinner. Seymour feels relieved when Susan suddenly says, "I'd like to pay my share of the expenses." At the same time, however, he also feels <u>embarrassed</u> that he feels relieved, and he therefore can't bring himself to admit that he <u>is</u> relieved. While Seymour is thinking all this over, Susan is puzzled by his silence. "Is something bothering you?" "No," he says, "nothing." Susan knows he's on a tight budget and she thought her offer would please him, but now she's afraid he's angry. She wonders if she perhaps hurt his feelings, and slowly, almost imperceptibly, she begins to close in order to protect herself against possible future disappointment.

about everything being for the best. And you wonder: do any of these people *know*?

Not even your mother seems to understand what you're going through. Tell her *your* problems and she might say, "So now you finally understand what *I've* had to go through."

DATE

"Have you put on weight?" Bradley asks on their second date. She says, "That hurts! Don't you understand I have feelings?" Brad insists there's no reason for her to feel hurt — and anyway, he thinks it's better to bring things like that out into the open. Melanie says, "Things like what??" and begins to cry. He feels like running and wonders whatever possessed him to invite her out a second time.

SEX BOOK

Amy brings home a book on sex and asks him to read it. He hides his embarrassment by saying, "What on earth do we need to read that stuff for?" She feels put down and hurt. What she says is, "I don't know what you're so mad about, I was just trying to improve things for both of us." He replies, "Who says that we need any help?" Both feel betrayed.

That's how your heart gets broken. Sometimes, one quarrel too many is enough to break your heart. Something goes out of you — sometimes for good.

FINANCES

Pam has always had to account to Mark for whatever she spends — an arrangement she never liked. Then she gets a part-time job and, wouldn't you know it, she immediately wants to open her own checking account and use the money as she wishes! He doesn't like that; he insists that both their salaries should be put into a joint account just as they've always done. "I don't agree with that," Pam says, "I want some financial independence." This makes Mark angry. "You didn't mind putting the money in a joint account when I was the only bread-winner," he says, "you're setting up a real double standard." "It may be a double standard," says Pam, "but that's the way I want it." When they look at each other, they both see defiance and rage.

Not that the *issue* being talked about is so important. Sometimes the issue hardly matters at all. But there's a limit

HOLDING ON

When Ted tells Claire he's thinking of moving out, she angrily says, "So that's all I mean to you!" Then she starts to sob, becomes filled with despair, and says: "I can't make it without you." When he tries to reassure her, saying, "You'll manage," she screams, "How can you be so above it all?" If he smiles because of her dramatic way of talking, she shouts "You're laughing at me!" Ted can't fathom her logic: one day she tells him no one has ever loved her as much as he does, the next day she will claim he doesn't care about her at all. To him this is all a game. He doesn't, however, know what to do about it other than to share his perceptions with her — which he knows she will regard as his being aloof, superior, and 'analytical.'

to someone's resilience. People are only so strong. So the issue being talked about isn't what does it. Sometimes just talking about something trivial, a small amount of money, and suddenly

HER FRIENDS

After her friends leave, she tells Matt he was rude and antagonistic to them. He says, "That's not true," and she says her friends thought so too. "Why don't you just tell the truth?" she demands. "Which is what?" he asks. "That you really want to alienate my friends!" "And why would I want to do that?" "Because you feel threatened by my even having friends!" "Really?" he says sarcastically, "and what am I so afraid of?" "Of losing control over me." Matt is really angry now and blurts out: "You're unbelievably paranoid, and as for your friends, most of them are nothing but tramps!"

your lover's heart is broken. And, once a heart is broken, can you ever mend it?

Hope sometimes postpones heartbreak. Hope keeps a lot of people going. Sometimes for many years. But there is a point where even hope dies.

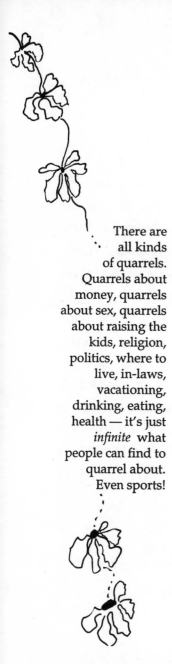

There are all kinds of quarrels. Quarrels about money, quarrels about sex, quarrels about raising the kids, religion, politics, where to live, in-laws, vacationing, drinking, eating, health — it's just *infinite* what people can find to quarrel about. Even sports!

FIGHT!

She: "You should have paid the credit card bill! When I went to charge, they wouldn't let me use it." He: "You're right, Jolene, I goofed." She: "Damn it, Clyde, don't you ever fight back?"

DOPE ADDICT?

Terry and Donna used to smoke dope together. Donna stopped when she got pregnant, but Terry continued and now he smokes almost every day. He's also started using cocaine at parties — he claims it helps him unwind. She wants him to stop but he gets defensive. "There's nothing wrong with marijuana," he says, "and coke's alright too if you know how to handle it." Donna doesn't want her child to grow up in this atmosphere but when she tries to talk with him about it, he simply yells at her, "Come on, get off my back, will you?!"

GARDEN

He: "I'd like you to help me in the garden." She: "What for, Gordy, _you_ never do any of the housework."

SEXUAL INITIATIVE

"I've made an interesting discovery," Jill says. "Oh," he says, "what's that?" "That whenever _I_ initiate sex, you never respond. Why is that?" Milton says she's imagining things. "You know it's true! Why won't you ever let _me_ be sexy? What are you so scared of?" "Who's scared?" he says, "I just don't like it when you're being sexually forward." So Jill gets angry and finally says "You're a male chauvinist pig!" "Look," he insists, "I want you to be responsive, but I certainly don't want you to be overbearing." This really irks her and she says, "Well, what about my needs? Or do you just want me to wait until _you're_ in the mood?"

All these quarrels express themselves in different ways — with hot anger, cold withdrawal, rivers of tears, violence...

But at bottom, there is one thing that characterizes all quarrels. And that is **The Blame Game.**

POWER TRIP?

…*her job to pay the bills and balance the checkbook but she always said "Why won't you do it?" And it was always a source of friction between them because, as far as Rick was concerned, she'd always mess everything up. One day he decides that from now he'll pay the bills. But Joanne says "Wait a minute, Rick, don't I have anything to say about it?" "You've been complaining for years," he says, "and I've had enough." "You and your power trips!" she says, "you're making a completely arbitrary decision without even consulting me," and she starts to sob. He says "Hey, what's really going on, Joanne?" She goes on sobbing and he suddenly feels sick.*

The Blame Game is also known as Fault-Finding, Nit-Picking, Making The Other Wrong, Criticizing, Bitching, Complaining, Whining, and Seeing The Mote In The Other's Eye. We play the Blame Game because we have expectations. And why do we have expectations? Because we think

COMPANIONSHIP

Polly looks forward to his getting home from work. She likes to talk things over with him and calls it 'visiting.' But as soon as Martin walks in the door he turns on the TV, reads his paper, and tells the kids they're making too much noise. "Don't you want to kiss a little and talk to me?", Polly asks. "No," he says, "I've worked hard and I'm tired. I don't want to be your sounding board, and I'd appreciate your not trying to make me feel guilty." "Don't you think I'm entitled to a little attention?" she asks. "Look," Martin says, "I don't want an argument, I don't want drama, all I want is a quiet evening, now is that too much to ask?" Leaves her speechless.

we *need* the other and think we are dependant on the other. That's why we have expectations.

And when our expectations are not fulfilled we feel angry. And underneath the anger we feel let-down. We get angry because someone has

SPAGHETTI

She: "I want to throw a dinner party and serve Cornish Game Hen." He: "That sounds too expensive — why don't we have spaghetti instead?" She: "I would <u>never</u> serve spaghetti at a dinner party!" He: "What's wrong with spaghetti? My mother always served spaghetti!" She: "Anyway, if you won't give me the money, I'll simply cancel the arrangements and tell everyone that you can't afford it."

TURNED ON.

Diane is more attentive to him in public than at home. So he asks, "How come?" She says: "It's the way you dress, darling, that turns me on. I <u>like</u> being seen with you!" He: "What turns you on, Diane, me, or the impression I make?" She says, "Oh, don't analyze everything, Jimmy! It's so boring. Just enjoy!" He now realizes he feels weird. He knows something is wrong, but what is it?

let us down. If we allowed ourselves to really *feel* let-down, we would feel hurt. Feeling our hurt is something we don't like, so we prefer

NOT CLEAR

She says, "Earl, you're putting words in my mouth again!" "I'm quite aware of that, Shirley," he replies, "and the reason is that what you say never makes sense."

UNFORGETTING

"You've never forgiven me, have you?" She: "I don't know what you're talking about." "Oh yes you do, Mary," he says, "and you never have forgiven me, ever." She says, "Well, I've tried." "Look," he asks, "what's trying? 'Trying' isn't enough! Do we really have to go on like this?" She for a while says nothing, then she says, "Warren, I just can't forget." He asks, "How long are you going to go on punishing me for something I've regretted for years?"

to get angry instead. Blaming the other, finding fault with the other, isn't pleasant — but at least it's less uncomfortable than feeling hurt. We know, from experience that it feels better to blame than not to blame. If we don't blame someone, we feel worse.

Blaming the other, focusing on the other — on our husband, wife, lover, friend, on someone or something outside of us — keeps us from becoming aware of how we really feel inside.

FLIRTATION

It's Christmas and they go to his company's office party. There's lots of good cheer and the man who's bucking for his job makes a pass at her. She enjoys the attention and flirts back. Later, driving home, he says: "Did you have to flirt like that? I thought it was sickening." She says: "Jeff, I don't know what you're talking about, and if you don't want me to have a little fun occasionally, maybe you'd better not invite me out again."

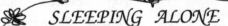

SLEEPING ALONE

Don tells her he can't get a good night's sleep when they sleep in the same bed. This upsets Kim: "You mean you want to sleep alone instead of with me?" Don goes into a long explanation regarding his health needs and then feels increasingly resentful because she doesn't seem to care. Meanwhile she feels hurt because he doesn't want to sleep with her.

Is all this quarreling really worth it? Does it get us anywhere? You can be victorious in almost any other kind of fight, but can you be victorious in a lovers' quarrel? In a lovers' quarrel, both are losers.

LATE NIGHT MOVIE

Jerry often gets out of bed to watch the late night movie on TV. She has never said anything about it, but one night she starts to cry and says, "I feel so abandoned when you do that." He says: "Aren't you being a little hyper-sensitive? It wouldn't bother me if you got out of bed to watch TV." Laura doesn't answer. He caresses her absent-mindedly for a few moments, but now he feels ill-at-ease. To him this incident means that she's unreasonable and over-emotional — and that scares him. What the incident means to her is that he doesn't love her nearly as much as she loves him.

Human relationships can be a great school. What do they teach? They teach you that the other has to be considered and that the other is different. They teach you many things, and ultimately they teach you that

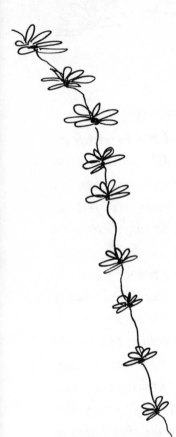

BIG TALKER

Ever since Sue's known him, Paul has been telling her about his grandiose schemes. Each one of which ends with their becoming fabulously rich. He's written one business plan after another, but nothing tangible ever seems to happen. A moment comes when she's had it. "I can't stand all your big talk anymore," she says. "Big talk? What big talk??" Sue realizes he doesn't even know what she's talking about. "I can't go on living like this!" she cries. "I want you to either get one of these projects off the ground or get a job!" "Job," he says, as though it's a dirty word, "I'd shrivel up and die on a job! They wouldn't even know what to do with a man like me." She appreciates Paul's talent and wants to be supportive, but she's now at a point where she's tired of working and wants results.

leaning on the other can be dangerous. They teach you not to depend on the other, because when you depend on the other

STATUS STRUGGLE

They're choosing a restaurant and he says "Let's go to Victor's," but she says "Nobody eats at Victor's anymore, let's go to the Champlain." Once in the restaurant, he tells her "The Beef Strogonoff is the best in town. And you really ought to try the brussels sprouts, they're generally not available this time of year." She says, "Thanks for the advice, but I prefer the trout with asparagus." "I wasn't giving you advice," he says, "I was trying to be helpful!" "You were giving me advice," she says, "and I really don't need it." "If that's the way you feel," he says angrily, "order whatever you damn please!"

you weaken yourself. Once you learn that, you learn to be careful with your expectations. Because expectations

ILLNESS

Whenever she gets sick, Tammy expects sympathy and tender loving care. Stuart is the opposite: when he's sick he likes being left alone and, what's more, he thinks being left alone is essential if you want to get better. And he doesn't understand why he should give her sympathy! "As far as I'm concerned," he says, "you caused yourself to get sick smoking cigarettes and eating junk food." When she hears she isn't going to get the sympathy she feels she deserves, Tammy says, "You don't love me." Stuart counters that his urging her to cut out junk food, cigarettes, sugar and milk is definite proof that he _does_ love her, and how come she can't see that?

are so often a source of friction. One person says "You promised" and the other person makes excuses. And then both become very self-righteous.

YOU DECIDE

He: "What do you want to do tonight, dear?" She: "I don't know darling, what would you like to do?" He: "You decide." She: "I'd rather leave it up to you." He: "Well, you know me, I'm easy to please." She: "Why don't you pick something you really want to do?" He: "But there's nothing I really..." She: "Well how about..." He: "Oh, let's just forget about it!" She: "We might as well, after all, it's late." Not a quarrel exactly, more like a stand-off. And it happens so often, Bill and Maxine have lost count. "We never fight," they say. Of course they don't; they bore each other to death instead.

Have you seen self-righteous people? The world could collapse around them and they'd still insist they were right.

Self-righteous people are behind all the wars, all the inhuman rules and regulations. We can hardly imagine what the world would be like if everyone *stopped* being self-righteous — our guess is that the world would bask in an ocean of love!

WHOSE GADGET?

Fred hits the ceiling when he discovers Jo's been using their brand new VCR — which he bought to tape his sports events — to record her soap operas. "Why didn't you ask me how it works?" he asks. "Because I'm smart enough to figure that out for myself," she says. "Besides, you always act as though every gadget we get is your exclusive property, and that really gets my goat."

FUR COAT

Shortly after Dolly got married, her mother decided she needed a fur coat. Dolly's husband couldn't afford one, so the mother-in-law gave her one on the first possible occasion. He looked on, a forced smile on his face, pleased and humiliated at the same time. The coat will figure in family photographs for years to come. It is the first rift between them.

When people first get into a relationship, they've often been yearning for one. They've been eager for companionship, whether with the opposite sex or the same sex, eager for some TLC, some tender loving care.

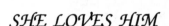

SHE LOVES HIM

Natalie shows her love by cooking gourmet meals. Of course they invite friends and business associates, and that's good for his career. The trouble is he's getting fat and he's been warned he needs to reduce his cholesterol level. "You've got to cut out rich food," his doctor says, "we need to lower your blood pressure." But she 'loves him' and says: "Dave, I want to make you one of those marvelous meals you enjoy so much." He wonders: does she _really_ love him? Or is it that she simply likes to display her culinary skills? These thoughts depress him. She asks, "What's wrong, darling? Why aren't you happy?" "Oh," he says, "just one of those moods." "You are moody," she smiles, "well, let me fix you a nice dinner!"

Most people come into relationship with high hopes and dreams. And they're excited because they've found someone who is going to fulfill those dreams. Then they have their first disagreement. It's not a quarrel yet, it's only a disagreement. They're still trying to be nice to each other, trying to be

MONEY

Brenda wants them to go on a really nice vacation, preferably to Greece. Pete doesn't. "Why should we go half-way around the world," he asks, "to a country where you can't even read the road signs? Why can't we just drive to the beach and go camping?" But Brenda isn't fooled. "Is putting money in the bank the only thing you're interested in?" she asks. "Don't you ever want to do anything exciting?" "Heck," Pete says, unwilling to admit to his concern about finances, "life can be just as exciting as you want it to be right around here." "Doing what?" Brenda asks, "playing monopoly?"

understanding and courteous. So a lot of their feelings don't get expressed, and afterwards, frequently, there's some resentment.

And then one day they have their first real quarrel. It's nothing as yet compared to the quarrels that are still on the horizon but it is a quarrel. They're not just discussing;

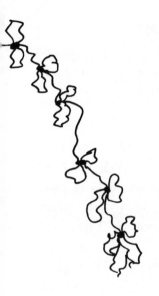

DISHES
She: "I'd like you to help me with the dishes." He: "That's the wife's job, the men in my family don't do dishes."

OH, I FORGOT!
Anne has been away for several days at a conference, and they celebrate her return with wine, love-making and food. The next morning he says, "Oh, I forgot — your father had a stroke two nights ago and he's in the hospital." Anne is shocked and furious and says, "For goodness sakes, Tom, why didn't you get in touch with me?!" He says, "There was nothing you could have done, they say it's too late." "But you could have called me!" "What for?" he says, "Anne, there was nothing you could do." To her, he is showing amazingly callous disregard for how she feels about her father.

they now admit to some real disappointment. Maybe they even get angry. That's the next phase: they start expressing feelings they haven't ever expressed before, feelings they never even knew they had. They express feelings they've never expressed before and

EASY

Gene: *"Don't complicate things. Just do whatever I tell you, and everything will be fine."* Guess what Rhoda did?

TIT-FOR-TAT

They're nobody's fools, they don't let anybody put one over on them or push them around, and they deal with problems by getting even. If Kevin loses money playing poker, Cindy claims her right to spend an equal amount of money on clothes. When she (against his wishes) invites her family to stay with them for a few days, he (against her wishes) goes to Las Vegas for a few days. They insist on their respective rights first and foremost, regardless of what happens. Sometimes, each feels they would like this tit-for-tat game to come to an end, but how can they end it without giving in?

they try to work them through. And if they can work some of these feelings through — and they hardly know what that means at this point, 'working feelings through' — then the bond between them gets deeper and they become more committed. Then deeper issues

IN AGREEMENT

Walter discussed with her at considerable length the pros and cons of buying a house. He thought he and Julia were in agreement, and he's shocked when he discovers that's not so. "But why," he asks, "didn't you say anything?" "Because I'm afraid of speaking up," Julia says, "and anyway, I couldn't really follow what you were talking about." He looks at her in amazement. "But I discussed everything with you, I asked for your input..." "You did," she says. "I asked if you had any questions..." "I was just afraid to speak up," she says. "I didn't realize any of this was so important to you." He feels sick to his stomach. What can they do to clear all this up?

come up, and once again, they either work things through or go their own way. That's how a relationship gets built. That's how trust develops.

The disappointment and the anger and the hurt all get transformed in some way, and it's nothing less than miraculous.

WHO WILL?

She: "Don't tell me what to do!" He: "If I don't tell you what to do, who will?"

RED FLAG

He got a well-paying job because of her father who's a V.I.P. Now they have everything they could ever want but Ross feels guilty because he didn't make it on his own. Ginger knows this, and whenever she gets really mad, she says "Where would you be if it weren't for me?" Even if she doesn't actually say the words, he can pick up on the energy, and it's like waving a red flag in front of a bull. She says she can't help it, and he ought to get over it. He sometimes agrees, but whenever that vibe of "Where would you be if...?" comes from her, Ross goes into a silent angry sulk and that means there may be bad medicine between them for days.

Strife is the cement that forges deep bonds. Without it, you don't know who you're with. Without some fighting, the other person remains an unknown — unknown in all kinds of ways, an unknown quantity and an unknown quality. It's only when you fight that you discover who you're really living with and who *you* really are.

HELP

She is in the helping professions, she enjoys being helpful, and he likes being helped. So at age 33, Joel decides to go back to school while Bonnie supports him. Their first fight is when he spends money on something she considers unnecessary. Joel deals with her objections by saying "I didn't realize I wasn't supposed to do that" and sulking. He then begins meticulously to ask for her OK every time he needs to spend money. This soon annoys her because he does it even when the expenditures are tiny and absolutely essential. One day Bonnie screams at him: "You stupid jerk, can't you understand I'm trying to help you?!"

But fighting is also demoralizing, debilitating, disheartening. It can be experienced as a terrible wound. After you've talked and talked and nothing has helped, you give up. You realize you love the other person, but you can't reach them. So you resign yourself to not talking. You recognize that you can't talk to your partner, and your partner feels the same way. And after a while of this, you feel as though you're living in a grave.

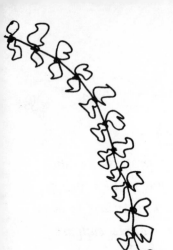

NO EXCUSES

Charles knows that when he gets home, Lois is going to complain about any number of things, including his being late for dinner and the fact that he didn't phone her all day. Since he can't stomach her complaining, he decides to get the jump on her. So as soon as he walks in the door, he exclaims in a loud voice, "How come the garage was left open?" This rattles her and she immediately feels guilty. "I don't know how it happened," she starts to say, but Charles interrupts and says, "Just own it, will you, I can't stand excuses!" He waits until she's about to say something and then says: "Why can't you ever admit anything??" By this time Lois is numb and doesn't know what hit her.

You suspect your lover is playing some sort of game but when you ask them about it, they say they're not. They're even hurt or annoyed that you think so. So you don't get confirmation. And after a while you start to wonder if you're crazy or if they are.

HIS VOICE

... on the phone for fifteen minutes. When he hangs up, Nan immediately says, "Who was that?" "That was Steve." "What did he want?" "Oh," he says, "it's not important." "Why don't you want to tell me?" "Because it was confidential." Nan doesn't say another word and starts pouting. She pouts and pouts until he can't stand it anymore. He finally tries to talk to her about it and asks, "Do you really expect me to tell you something that was said to me in confidence?" She says, "That's not what upset me! I was hurt because of your voice." "What was wrong with my voice?" "Your voice," she says, "was so harsh and unloving." "Well," he says, "I felt annoyed! Why do you insist I tell you something I obviously don't want to?" This remark, of course, sets her off on a new round of pouting.

In the beginning you don't tell your lover everything you think. You keep some reserve. But after a while that gets harder and harder. Gradually you begin to blurt out things you would never have said before. You don't, in fact, care anymore what you say and what you don't. Curiously, the distance

CRAZY

She: "You're driving me crazy! What are you <u>doing</u> with me?" He: "Just relax! If you didn't try to figure everything out, you wouldn't have any problems."

COLD HANDS

It's been a long day, and they've been looking forward to going to bed. When they finally do, Janice puts her arms around him — and he jumps because her hands are icy cold. "Don't touch me," he says, "until your hands are warm!" "Oh," she says, without taking her hands away, "are you really all that fragile?" Luke is indignant and says: "I feel really disregarded when you do that." She says: "I'm not disregarding you! What's the matter with you?? I just wanted to caress you, where's your sense of humor?"

between you and your lover diminishes, but is that good? You certainly don't know if you like it or if you don't.

Puzzled, perplexed, embarrassed, you don't know what to do, and then somebody says talk to a counselor or a minister. So you try that, and there's certainly a change, but again you don't know if you like it. Now there's a third party in the relationship, this *therapist* to whom you're saying

YES, DEAR

He has talked to Margo for hours telling her he wants an equal relationship. But all he gets from her is "Yes, dear, I understand — I'm supposed to be an equal partner to you in this relationship." As far as he can tell, this is how she talks whenever she wants to get his goat ("Yes, John — whatever you say — just tell me what I'm supposed to do") and it sends him up the wall, especially since she always seems to do things exactly the way she wants. So he accuses her of 'passive aggression' and she insists she doesn't understand what he's talking about. "Can't we just love one another, John?" she asks. This leaves him apoplectic and unable to say a word.

all kinds of personal things, and that feels odd. And slowly you realize you can never go back to the way things used to be when there were just the two of you. *So* many people give you advice, and frequently the advice is in terms of 'should' and 'shouldn't.' Everybody says you and your lover are supposed to get closer, but sometimes you wonder if maybe you haven't gotten *too* close. Is it possible that some sort of borders or limits are

TIRED

He: "I'm really tired." She: "Ian, you're <u>always</u> tired." He: "And you, Sandy? You're always horny!"

WEDDING BELLS?

"What are you thinking?" Ray asks her. Eileen answers: "I'm wondering what it would be like if we got married." Ray: "Don't you ever think about anything else?" Eileen: "What's wrong with thinking about marriage?" Ray: "Nothing, except I'm not the marrying kind." Eileen: "Well you don't have to get all tight and closed! There's nothing so terrible about marriage. And anyway, you wanted me to tell you what I was thinking, I told you, and now you're mad!"

needed in a relationship? Or do you really have to tell another person everything you think and feel? Is that really healthy?

But you're aware that you do need to talk, so you start talking to other people. After a while you notice that though it's nice to get some sympathy and understanding, that seems to take you even further away from your lover. So it's almost like "damned if you do and damned if you don't." What kind of weird game is this, anyway?

SUNDAY SEX

Every Sunday morning it's the same blessed thing — he is turned on and wants to make love. And Holly feels torn in two because, meanwhile, the children are getting frantic and want their breakfast! For ages now, he has kept on saying he wants her to arrange for someone to look after the kids on Sunday mornings, but she says, "Don't be silly, Marvin, I couldn't make love to you with a stranger in the house!" "Look," he says, "we're entitled to a little privacy! We have needs too. There's got to be one day in the week when we can make love without hurrying!" The fact that Holly doesn't seem to be in any hurry to solve this problem leaves him feeling angry and frustrated.

You hear about books that may help and you start reading them. So many books, and they all tell you about how to relate to the one person in the world you know better than anybody else! And these books say all sorts of things.

Some say it's much better to view

CHURCH

It's Sunday morning and Dee wants them to go to church. "You can go if you want to," Phil says, "I don't feel like going." Dee says, "It's important for a family to all go to church together." Phil says he doesn't see why. "Well what about the children? What kind of example are you giving them?" "A darn good one! At least they know their Dad isn't a hypocrite." "What?" "Don't you see, I'd be like all those other hypocrites if I sat in that church when my heart wasn't really in it." She starts to say "But..." when Phil trumps her and says "Dee, do you think God wants a person to be a hypocrite?" Dee can't argue with him on that, but still, the fact that he won't go to church upsets her deeply.

marriage as not so much a source of fulfillment as a learning experience. That when the first differences of opinion come, that's not to be seen as a betrayal of the relationship but rather as something that's expected, something that will further "growth." And you wonder why a normal grown-up adult, like yourself, would need constantly to be 'growing.'

MOTHER

After his mother's visit, Henry feels Nina doesn't care about him; Nina meanwhile feels _he_ doesn't care about _her_. But what he says is: "How could you talk to my mother like that?" while she replies, angry: "I guess your mother means more to you than I do!"

BIRTH CONTROL

"I'm tired of getting pregnant and I want you to have a vasectomy," Cynthia insists. "Okay, okay," Norman says, but he keeps putting it off because the truth is he doesn't really want one. After a while Cynthia gets annoyed. "What's the matter?" she asks, "is Mommy's hero afraid a little operation like that is going to affect his manhood?" "I sure am," he says. This really irritates her. "You don't care what happens to _my_ body, Norman," she says, "just as long as _you_ don't feel any discomfort."

The ways of love are very unpredictable. Sometimes people yearn for love without finding it

MOVIE

He: "Do you want to go to a movie or don't you?" She: "I don't know." He: "Well make up your mind, Jenny, otherwise we'll just waste the whole evening." She: "Stop badgering me, you ass, I don't want to be pinned down!"

"<u>DO</u> SOMETHING!"

When they have sex, he comes too soon and that leaves her feeling frustrated and angry. "If you really loved me," she says, "you wouldn't be in such a hurry. You'd wait for me." "I'm doing the best I can," he claims; to which she coldly replies, "I don't believe you." "Alice, I can understand your being disappointed," he says, "but it's not my fault and you don't have to be angry." She remains angry and continues to insist that he "do something." Instead of 'doing something,' he gradually loses all interest in sex. By the time they decide to talk to a marriage counselor, they're hardly able to talk at all.

and sometimes they simply fall into love without even looking for it. But regardless of whether they've yearned for it, planned for it, or just fallen into it,

PAYCHECK

She: "George, where's your paycheck?"
He: "They haven't made it out yet." She:
"Well, you ought to go to your boss and
complain!" He: "I can't do that." She:
"Why not, George? Are you going to let
them walk all over you??"

TOILET PAPER

He: "Judy, there's no toilet paper in the
bathroom." She: "Well, go get some,
Neil, I'm busy!" He: "Well why isn't
there?" She: "Because there isn't — if you
want some toilet paper, put it there
yourself." He: "But that's your job!"
She: "Neil, don't tell me how to run this
house! I don't tell you how to do your
job." He: "But I'm at the office all day."
She: "Well, don't you wipe yourself when
you're at home? So if you want toilet paper,
do something about it! He: "Judy, I was just
calling it to your attention, I wasn't telling
you what to do." She: "You most certainly
were too telling me what to do!"

lovers know that
love feels
wonderful.
That's something
you don't need to
be told.

SHE UNDERSTANDS

His wife confronts him about the affair he's having. He: "Why can't you be interested in what I think and feel? She is!" She: "Every woman is like that when she's trying to get a man!" He: "She's genuinely understanding. And you are being very destructive!" Stubbornly, Chris continues to argue that Eva is wrong — even though, in his heart, he suspects she may be right.

Loving someone is wonderful, and it's wonderful to be in love. Everything is so delightful, and you feel so exhilarated that you can't imagine things will ever be different. And yet things are different or at least *get* different — very quickly!

BACKSEAT DRIVER

Cliff and Marlene are driving in downtown Detroit and she, as usual, is telling him what to do. There's nothing going on that hasn't gone on countless numbers of times. But today, for no discernible reason at all, he decides he's had enough. He stops, puts on the hand brake, shuts off the ignition, and gets out without even looking at her. Then, totally ignoring her screams, he walks off leaving her stuck in traffic — and unable to drive a car.

TELEPHONE

He: "You call me up too often, Shelley. I can't get my work done!" Shelley: "OK Bruce. If that's the way you feel about it, I'll never call you again!"

NEW CAR

Megan keeps telling him they need some new living room furniture. Instead, Robert buys her a fancy red sports car with a five-speed gear shift. She doesn't know what to say, especially since she can't drive a car that isn't an automatic. "What about the furniture?" she asks. He gets annoyed and says, "A lot of women would be delighted to get a fancy car like that, and all you can do is nag me about furniture. Honey, we don't even _need_ new furniture!" "Do my wishes matter, Robert," Megan asks, "or don't they?"

Lovers tend to start fighting — sometimes very soon after they first get together. Of course, some people have never known what it is to be in love, and if you haven't, you may be able to have a smoothly functioning relationship instead. A kind of rational business operation. But if you _are_ an authentic

FLOWERS

They squabble about something, bicker, fight, and then Denise locks herself in the bathroom. "Let me in," Sam calls through the door, "I want to talk to you!" "Well," she says, "I don't want to talk to you!" He finally gets so mad he breaks the door down. Then he starts slapping her and telling her what a bitch she is. "Don't ever do that again!" he yells, hitting her so hard she gets really frightened. The next day Sam brings her flowers and tells her how terribly sorry he is. She falls into his arms, enormously relieved; five minutes earlier, she realizes, she was thinking of leaving him! P.S. This will be their almost daily pattern for the next five years, but they don't yet know it.

lover, quarreling is just about inevitable. It goes with the turf. We once asked a well-married friend of ours whether he had fought with his wives. "Yes," he smiled, "I did, but not nearly as much as I should have." And he reminded us of an important finding: that the way a couple deals with conflicts is the single most important factor in the success of a relationship.

NEW DRESS

"I know you don't like my new dress," Abby says and pouts. He insists it's a lovely dress. She asks, "Do you really like it?" He says he does. She says: "I mean really?" "Yes, I really do." "Well," she says, "you don't _sound_ as though you really mean it." Andrew is now furious and ready to explode and he shows it through his body language, even though he doesn't say a word. Abby says: "You're always angry at me." They both begin to feel misunderstood and depressed and wonder how they ever managed to get themselves into such a mess. What can they do to reach out to each other?

You can deal with conflict by shoving it under the rug. You can deal with conflict by pretending it doesn't exist. You can deal with conflict by overpowering the other person —

SEXUAL BLISS

Just hearing Brent's voice is enough to turn Kay on. In her whole life she has never experienced anything like it. The trouble is he's unpredictable: she never knows when he's going to want to see her. If she says, "When am I going to see you?" he gets annoyed. She suspects Brent is having sex with a friend of hers, but if she asks him about it, he gets very nasty and withdraws all that wonderful energy. Kay feels that to be with him, she has to smile and say "Yes" to everything. They hardly ever talk. She keeps it all inside but one day she 'loses it' and starts sobbing. He looks at her as though she's positively demented.

— regardless of whether you do it with a club or by sweet-talking them into oblivion. No conflicts will ever arise if you hug and kiss them enough and if you persistently talk sweetly; that's one philosophy. We know people who don't even *hear*

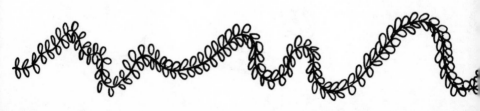

GAY?

...and all seems to be going well when dear old Jim, a former high school buddy of his, turns up for a visit. They're laughing and hollering, reminiscing about old times. Stacy feels left out but she reprimands herself for being so possessive. Then, a few days later, Jim reveals he's gay, and soon her husband shocks her by telling her he finds Jim 'intriguing.' "Intriguing?" she says, "what do you mean?" "Well, I admire him for having the courage to admit what he is." "But you don't mean you're attracted to him, do you?" "I don't know what I feel," he says. "I always liked Jim, and maybe I liked him more than I thought I did." Stacy is numb; finally she gets red in the face and tells him, with great anger, "I have never been so humiliated in my life!"

remarks they don't want to hear. They're convinced that anything that may possibly lead to friction must be tuned out. They insist on nothing but sweet talk; they think that's positive. They're right up to a point:

REASSURANCE

Kirsten frequently asks Richard for reassurance about her abilities and appearance. He thinks the world of her and repeatedly tells her she's wonderful. Yet he gets dejected because she constantly seems to need more and more reassurance. He also notices that if ever he suggests that she do something a little differently, she claims he's criticizing her. He feels she really doesn't want to know what he thinks and feels. This thought saddens him. "You don't want genuine feedback," he says one day. "You just want me to function as a kind of rubber stamp." "I can't believe," Kirsten says, "that you would ever actually say something as nasty as that!"

all the sweet-talking lovey-dovey stuff *is* great — but unfortunately, it doesn't last forever. Conflicts need to be dealt with. If you don't deal with them,

NEWLY MARRIED

They're newly married. She: "Darling, I need some money." He: "For what?" She: "For fingernail polish and deodorant." He: "Honey, you don't really need all that — you don't need fingernail polish, you only need deodorant."

SEXLESS

Their marriage has been without sex for about a year, and she keeps hoping that will change. Then one evening Dennis doesn't come home. When he finally does show up, about six in the morning, he's beaming. Colleen screams: "You've been with a woman!" "Yes, I have," he admits, "but that doesn't mean I don't love you." He's radiant and she's in agony. "But why don't you ever want to make love with me?" she says. "I don't know," he answers, "that's just the way it is." "You murderer!" she screams, "I work my knuckles to the bone for you and all you do is laugh at me!"

they gather momentum until one day nothing can stop them, and then they thunder down on you like an avalanche.

OTHER WOMAN

...*told her he was going to divorce his wife and marry her, and she always believed him. He kept postponing though, and then one day he told her he couldn't go through with it. "What do you mean, you can't?" she said. "I don't know," he said, "I just can't." She shakes with emotion and says: "How could you do this to me?" He says: "Harriet, look, I'm terribly sorry, I thought you'd understand." Still shaking, she says: "Well, I don't understand! I don't understand at all! Why do I always have to be so understanding?!?" "Look," he says and tries to hold her, but she refuses. "You've been stringing me along," she screams. "The only person you really care about is yourself!"*

What does learning to deal with conflicts mean? One thing it means is understanding that a lovers' quarrel does not have to be the end of the world. That lovers can disagree and argue and get mad and the love

ILLUSION?

She: "I have really deep feelings for you, Morris."   He: "Feelings aren't everything, Irene. Frankly, I think you're just laboring under an illusion."

RIDICULOUS

Wendy got very emotional on their last date and said things she later regretted. So she calls him up a week later to apologize. She says, "You must have thought I behaved ridiculously, didn't you?" Doug says, "No, not at all, I didn't think you were ridiculous, I thought you were just upset." Wendy is suddenly furious about his calm tone of voice. Before she's thought it over, she says, "Then you must consider me ridiculous <u>now</u> for thinking you considered my behavior ridiculous <u>then</u>! And what do you mean by saying I was 'just' upset? Don't you ever get upset?" Doug can't seem to get out from under regardless of what he does.

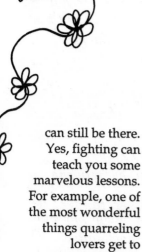

can still be there. Yes, fighting can teach you some marvelous lessons. For example, one of the most wonderful things quarreling lovers get to experience is the sequel to when you yell at your partner or even hang up on them

SWITCHEROO

Jessie puts Aaron on a pedestal and thinks he's wonderful — some of the time. The rest of the time she thinks he's mean, nasty, cruel, and horrible. He notices that this switch occurs whenever he wants something. "Look," he says, "I can't be supportive all the time!" "Why not?" she asks. "Because," he replies, "I also have needs!" "Of course you do," she says, "but _my_ needs are more important!"

SUBMISSIVE?

Helga exasperates him by refusing to say what it is she wants. Instead of speaking up, she acts as though she's the helpless victim of his domination. "I really want you to be more assertive," he says. "I'll try," she promises, but again and again she behaves as though she has to submit to his wishes. "I don't know what kind of game you're playing," he says. "I'm not playing any kind of game," she insists. What now?

when you're on the phone. That's a nightmarish moment when it happens the first time, but then you discover, when you meet your lover again (still mad, in all probability)

NO SEX UNLESS...

He offers to buy her a sports car. So they go to the showroom and she insists she wants the most expensive model! He says "Come on, Vera, be reasonable!" and she says, "I'm very reasonable!" That night, when he wants sex, she says "No!" — and she sticks to it. He gets so mad he says: "You're just like a hooker; you use sex to get what you want!" She says, "And what's wrong with that?" "It's immoral, that's what!" "Well," she says, "because you're a man, you earn more money than I could ever dream of making, and I consider that immoral." Instead of answering, he mutters obscenities and has fantasies of making her grovel like a dog.

— well, it's this way: she looks at him, he looks at her, and suddenly everything is all right again. That's a wonderful experience! And there's

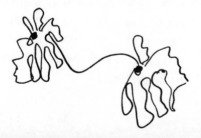

PROPERTY

He: "Where's our credit card?" She: "It's in my purse." He: "I'll go get it." She: "Don't you go through my purse! That's my private property." He: "When you're married, Sally, you don't _have_ any private property."

UPSET

During a small dinner party at her house, June gets an upsetting phone call. Seeing how upset she is, their friends try to comfort her. They encourage her to talk about her feelings and give her heartfelt advice. June seems to be genuinely appreciative of their concern, but the next morning she tells Wayne she felt humiliated. "They were awful," she says, "I felt they were skinning me alive and telling me I'm not supposed to be the way I am." This baffles him. "I didn't get that impression," Wayne says, "I thought they were doing their best to be helpful." She cries and says: "And I feel you put them up to this because you want me to be different!"

no way you could have had it without that lovers' quarrel. That's why a lot of people do fight — because there's nothing like

CATASTROPHE

Tony sees catastrophe in everything — an unexpected phone call, a meeting that was called off, etc. His reaction is to rave, rant, and claim people are against him. The latest is that the I.R.S. is questioning a tax return he filed three years ago. "There's nothing anybody can do once the I.R.S. goes after you!" he proclaims, shaking with fear and rage. "If they're out to get you, you've had it!" Mary Lou thinks he's overreacting. "They're only asking you to discuss a return," she says, "you don't have to assume the worst." "Don't tell _me_ how to be," Tony snaps at her, "I'm emotional, I've got blood in my veins." "Well," she responds, "you don't always have to act as though the world is coming to an end!"

the thrill of making up. If you've never done anything bad, how can you ever experience the joy of being forgiven? You really can't experience making up without first having a quarrel. Some things simply go together.

Amnesia seems to seize the brain after a quarrel. Which is a great pity, because if you can outline the dynamics of a quarrel and reconstruct lovers' quarrels the way we have in this book, you are on your way out of the woods.

SEX MANIAC?

"He's always after me," Jane tells her friends, "He always wants more. He's a sex fiend." A friend of hers shares this information with Bryan and he is amazed. "How can she say that? It's not true at all! Touch is much more important to me than sex." "It is?" says their mutual friend, astonished, "Then what's the problem between you two?" "The real problem is she's so tense she never feels like just being quiet and caressing. She wants to _talk_ all the time." One day Jane finds out what he's been saying. "What do you mean," she screams at him, "telling everybody I talk all the time? What kind of thing is that to say to people?" Bryan now feels enraged, guilty, and depressed. Would it be better, he wonders, to murder her or to commit suicide?

OUT OF SYNC

Stanley and Elizabeth say they love each other, but they're always putting each other down. They're almost never tender, they're always on the go, and they engage in an ongoing habit of subtly — or not so subtly — disparaging each other (they think that's funny, and they tend to horselaugh about it a lot). Despite all this, they continue to insist they have a good relationship. "Our marriage is as good as any, and some marriages are a lot of worse." Occasionally they admit they simply don't know how to make their marriage more satisfying. "Something's better than nothing," he'll sigh in an unguarded moment, and she tells friends it's "better than being alone."

Some people, of course, remember lovers' quarrels in vivid detail. But what they remember is one-sided. It is a distortion of the original quarrel, not the true interaction. That is why these people are often clients in counseling. They are bitter or full of grief, or both, about the injustice of it all. And that kind of attitude doesn't help anyone. Fault-finding is a sure one-way ticket to either hell or the divorce court.

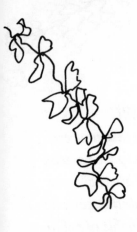

CLIP JOINT

At her apartment he had said, "Wherever you want to go." But when they sit down, Elliott looks at the menu and says, "This is a clip joint!" "So?" she says. "So let's get out of here!" "But you said we could go any place I wanted!" "Don't whine!" he says, spitting the words out, "I know what I said, you don't need to remind me, but this place costs an arm and a leg." Jennifer likes the place, she's hungry, and she was really looking forward to this date. Now she feels he's questioning her judgment and ruining their whole evening. Why is he being such a slime? She's not entirely sure, though, if it's her fault or his.

When you look around and observe humanity over a long period of time, it seems that even relationships that go on for years end with people having a falling out and quarreling.

Colleagues, political allies, brothers, business partners, all once committed to building something together, to a shared vision, to a beautiful dream

"DID YOU...?"

He's an over-achiever — everywhere, including the bedroom. So he frequently asks her, "Did you?" If she says she hasn't yet, he goes on working at it until she does. A seemingly perfect gentleman, he puts her satisfaction ahead of his. And whenever he himself comes first, he apologizes profusely. Exemplary behavior, isn't it? So consequently it's completely beyond him why Cathy so often seems dissatisfied. "Is there something you're unhappy about?" he asks. There is, but since she can't understand what it is, what can she say?

— and lo and behold, they're no longer even on speaking terms and it's a wonder if they don't want revenge. Isn't it amazing

GOD

She: "I want us to have another child." He: "We can't afford it." She: "God will provide." He: "Don't talk nonsense! You're being totally impractical, Lulu."

GOING OUT

...to a party where he hopes to meet people who could be helpful to him in business. Libby says, "I won't know anybody there." Mike says, "But honey, this is important!" Finally she agrees to come along, but when she isn't dressed when he's ready to leave the house, he gets mad. In the car she asks, "Why are you so angry?" He isn't really sure, but what he says is, "I can't stand your acting helpless all the time." This of course pours fuel on the fire. "I don't know what you're talking about," she says, "and besides, why did you make me come?" This gets him even more mad. Suddenly he says, "To hell with the party," turns the car around, and drives home. How soon do you think it will be before they can really talk?

how many friendships and relationships end after ten or even twenty years of joy, intimacy, harmony, solidarity... shipwrecked because of some unforeseen issue that results in dissension.

TROUBLE MAKER

She: "I'd like us to talk about why I'm not happy in this relationship." He: "Oh, Ginny, you're always trying to cause trouble!"

FRUSTRATED

Late at night. Asks her to come to bed. Wants to make love but doesn't say that. "I'll come to bed in a moment," she says, but then she spends 45 minutes in the bathroom 'getting ready.' 'Getting ready' means she's having beautiful sexual fantasies while he's increasingly impatient. By the time she does come to bed, he's annoyed, resentful and, what's more, half-asleep. Now it's she who tries to get him to make love, but by this time he's crotchety and says, "I'm not in the mood, and it's late, and I have to get up early." She starts to cry, at which point, of course, he gets even angrier, snatches up some of the covers, and goes to sleep in the other room.

Are there solutions to any of this? Do we all, sooner or later, have to quarrel with people who are dear to us? We think pure love is the solution. Love without

DENIAL

...*comes home one evening after visiting a friend. And gets the impression something's bothering her. And so he asks, "Is anything wrong, Angie?" "No," she insists, "nothing's wrong." He says, "You're angry. You are, you know. Did I do something that made you angry?" To which she says: "Why don't you, just for once, listen to what I say without trying to interpret my mood? You never listen to what I say, do you??" A fine kettle of fish! It's obvious Angie is angry, he knows she's angry, and she refuses to admit she's angry! He can't understand what's bothering her and she won't even admit anything is bothering her!*

conditions and expectations. And that isn't unrealizable; it doesn't mean *perfect* love or divine love. It simply means

EMBARRASSED

It's a beautiful Spring day and they're walking down the street. Lindy reaches for Larry's hand and suddenly feels flushed and crazy when he abruptly pulls his hand away. She doesn't say or do anything because, after all, they're in public and she doesn't want to cause a scene. When they get home she says, "How could you embarrass me like that? Don't you love me?" He says: "What are you talking about?" When she explains he says: "Don't tell me you're still concerned about *that*!? It's true I didn't like your making a display of our affections, but I forgot that long ago. I don't hold on to my anger the way you do!" What do you think Lindy is feeling after all that?

appreciating the other without conditions or qualifications, seeing something wonderful in the other and approving of that — enjoying the other without conditions. Don't you love your puppy without conditions? Don't you love a *baby* without conditions?

CREDIT CARD

Bob has asked Sarah not to spend so much money. Then he finds out she used their credit card to purchase some very lavish items. When he confronts her about this she says: "You've got dollar signs in front of your eyes! You're hung up on money; it's all you ever think about." He feels himself burning with humiliation and anger and says, "I guess you just don't care about me, do you?" "No," she says, "it's the other way around; you don't care about either of us — I want us to live a really beautiful life, and I guess you're too insecure to do that." They don't speak or go near each other again for what seems like ages.

Can't you love a *kitten* without conditions? And if you can do that, why couldn't you love your husband or wife or lover without conditions?

CHICKEN

She is exercising. He is cooking. He: "How do you want me to fix the chicken?" She: "Oh, never mind, I'll do it!" He: "Fine! OK. But why are you mad at me?" She: "Well, when I interrupt you, _you_ always get mad!"

Without conditions doesn't mean without demands. Sometimes we do need to make some demands of our lovers. That's very normal and natural. And we can withhold rewards from them, too — sometimes that's necessary to get what we want. We can withhold

BOOZE

After suffering silently for months, Karen asked, "Will you please not drink so much?" and Glenn said "Yes," and she thought everything was OK. And then one day she suddenly discovered the truth, which was that he was stashing booze in secret places and drinking more than ever. So she felt bitterly disappointed and angry and hurt. Wouldn't talk to him and still won't, except for what's strictly necessary. An old story, you say? Perhaps. But now, what can either of them say or do that will bring them closer together again?

KISS ME!

Liza reads, talks on the phone, and watches TV all day. When Barry comes home she says: "Kiss me!" He does and she says: "Not there!" Then, before he's had a chance to catch his breath, she says: "I wanted you to make love to me last night; why didn't you?" Barry starts to feel sick and wishes he would have stayed in the office.

ADDICTS

If Al suggests anything to Meg that will improve the way she does things, she responds by saying, "I guess I'm really awful," after which she gets depressed, withdraws, and overeats. This makes him wonder if communication with her is possible, a thought which discourages and depresses him. Gradually, he finds his drinking getting out of control.

the amount of time we spend with them or how much attention we give them. But hopefully, we will withhold the degree of our participation,

TOO TIRED

She: "I'll tell you why we don't have sex more often — because I run myself ragged taking care of this house!" He: "Well, <u>don't</u> work so hard! I keep on telling you the house doesn't have to be so perfect."

QUESTIONS

Becky very often asks him probing questions about his feelings, their finances, his intentions, the mortgage, etc. The message Carl gets is that she doesn't fully trust him. He says: "I always tell you the truth; why won't you believe me?" She says: "I do, but I need re-assurance." "Is that why you constantly give me the third degree?" Becky is shocked by this, cries, and says: "I don't! How can you be like that?" He: "Because you just won't trust me!" "I don't want to fight with you, Carl," she says. "Why do you always have to make an issue out of everything?"

our energy and our attention, and not our love. We may get angry at them, but we will not close our hearts to them. We will find ways to honor them even

MEN

She: "You are the most helpless man I've ever known!" He: "Boy, you must really enjoy hurting a guy's feelings!"

WONDERING

Trudy tells him that some friends of theirs are moving to Japan. Hank grunts assent while he reads his newspaper. Next day he comes home from the office and says, "Hey, I just heard that the Carlsons are moving to Japan." Trudy says, "Sweetheart, I told you that last night." He looks at her and says, "No you didn't." "Yes, I did," she replies, "you just don't remember." Each is left wondering if the other isn't losing his marbles. They're not angry, but an imperceptible gulf of mental reservation begins to form between them, and they start to express themselves cautiously rather than spontaneously.

when we are angry. We can clash with them on many issues just as long as our love for them is not an issue.

How do you arrive at unconditional love? By wanting to. By recognizing that you *are* capable of it. By recognizing that you *are* love at your core and that your anger is

FURY

They're lovers, and for three months it's sex, sex, sex. Then one day Jack meets someone else and tells Lillian he wants out. Next thing she turns up at his office and says, "We've got to talk. I feel absolutely desperate," and makes a scene. To keep her quiet, he promises he'll come to her house to talk things over. When he does, she tells him how unfair he's being: "I can't even sleep and it's your fault!" Then, after twenty minutes of ranting and raving and alternating rage with seductive sweetness, she suddenly says, "Oh God I love you!" and before he knows it, they're in bed and she has her tongue in his mouth. Each time he tries to break away her the same kind of thing happens. Finally he tells her, very decisively, that he doesn't want to see her any more — and discovers, one fine day, that 'someone' has thoroughly trashed his car with a baseball bat!

a residue of deep wounds that go far back in time. They were sore spots that your lover touched off almost accidentally. He or she probably didn't intend to hurt you. And even if he did, he must have had something in his past that hurt him or her so badly

FRIENDS

She: "OK — I'm not going to see you any more — that's what you want, isn't it, Sid?" He: "No, that's __not__ what I want! Why can't you ever hear what I'm saying? I want us to be friends, Doris, I just don't want you pulling on me like this all the time!"

FRANKENSTEIN

She spent months encouraging Ken to talk to her about his feelings. Then he began — and he hasn't stopped since! He now talks endlessly about himself: his fears, his hopes, his problems, etc. She discovers she doesn't like it, and frequently changes the subject. This makes Ken angry and he says: "You kept after me to talk about myself, it was __your__ idea, why don't you make up your mind?!" She defends herself by saying "I had no idea what you were really like."

that he needed to hurt others. You see, once you see all that, you can, if you choose, climb off your high horse and opt for a beautiful forgiving reconciliation to take place.

We have to admit, though, that we still fight. We do all those things that you do — we think almost everybody does for a very

NOT OKAY

Carrie is feeling bad about herself and thinking she does this wrong and that wrong, and maybe she's not good enough for anyone. So she asks him if he loves her and if she's OK and he says yes, he loves her and she is OK, but she thinks the __way__ he says it means he's just saying it to reassure her and maybe he doesn't really mean it. So she again says, "I know you love me, but am I the most important person in the world to you, the woman you always want to be with, and do you really think I'm OK?"   After being subjected to this for a while he gets exasperated and says he can't stand her always asking him for reassurance. This confirms her in her belief that she is __not__ OK, and she wonders what's wrong with her.

long time. But we're learning. We understand our fighting and ourselves better as we go along. So, since we haven't gotten over our own tendencies to fight, we're certainly not going to preach that you do. In fact, the more we've thought about it, the more we've wondered if fighting doesn't serve a purpose. It must; why else is it so prevalent? You see, fighting is not just your personal aberration. It may at times look like that, but that's part of the hype that you're the only one

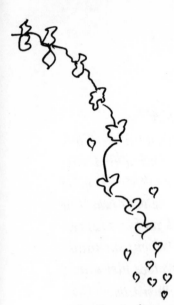

STOP

He: "Stop bugging me all the time, Nita!"
She: "Max, I wasn't bugging you!"

"DID YOU MISS ME?"

Mel comes home from work. Linda greets him at the door and asks: "I missed you today; did you miss me?" He: "I'm happy to see you now." She: "Yes, but did you miss me?" He (annoyed): "I don't like your asking me if I missed you." She: "But I want to know! Why should that make you angry?" He: "Well it does! I'm angry because I don't like your always asking me if I missed you." She: "Well, what's wrong with that if that's how I feel?" He: "You act as though I'm an awful person if I don't miss you, and that makes me angry." Once started, this can — and often does — go on for hours and even days.

who is out of step. Everybody is out of step! So quarreling is a natural phenomenon that involves all of humanity and a lot of other species as well. We're not sure exactly what the purpose is, but we think it's likely that there is one. Maybe lovers' quarrels are the primary method the Master Planner uses for reducing our egos and whittling us down to size. Don't you think that might just be possible?

INSTRUCTOR

Whenever he asks her anything, Joyce uses the occasion to give Hal some unasked for advice. If he asks "Where's the soap for the shower?" she answers by saying, "Soap isn't good for your skin if you use it every day." When he says he wants some dessert, she gives him a talk about sugar and proper nutrition. Often she adds, "Didn't you know that?" This begins to get on his nerves. One day he finally talks to her about all of this. She listens and says: "Don't you understand that you're being incredibly negative?" "Will you please," he says, "stop teaching me all the time?" He wonders if things will always be like that.

Some people, of course, don't fight. They live in perpetual harmony, and our guess is that many of them are probably bored. They sit on pools of stagnant energy. They probably don't get very close to one another, either.

In our experience, closeness and intimacy sometimes seem to require fighting. And there is nothing wrong with fighting, even frequently, as long as it results in growth and realization — in some insight, in understanding, in something constructive.

PREGNANT

Just when he's trying to break off their affair, Patty discovers she's pregnant. Will says: "I thought you were using birth control." She says: "I don't know what happened." "Well," says Will, "you'd better have an abortion, I'm not ready to be a father." Patty thinks this over for a few days and then tells him she won't. "If I have to," she says, "I'll bring up this child by myself." This makes him angry. She says: "I guess I was hoping having sex would bring us closer, but I think now you hate me." "Oh come on," he says, "you're imagining things, I certainly don't hate you," but he suspects that perhaps he does.

On the whole, we think occasionally fighting is probably better than never fighting. It's how underlying issues get exposed. It's how old wounds are brought to the surface so they can heal. Without at least some openness to fighting, everything just festers.

Do you know that terrible feeling when you're in a room with people and you can feel that horrible tension in the air that comes from unfought fights? Invisible fights that just sit there and ruin everything? Fighting may be ugly but at least it makes for some wonderful moments of truth.

MATING RITUAL

Arthur and Nicole have a strange mating ritual when they fight. They live on the eighth floor of a condo, and Art often gets so mad, he slams the door and storms out. Nicole likes that because that's how she knows he loves her. So his storming out makes her feel affectionate! If she can now get to him before he's gotten into the elevator, she pulls him back into their apartment and they make up — sometimes for hours. If she isn't quick enough, Art rides the elevator down to the first floor, gets into the car, and stews for an hour or two before he comes home. Then he's glum for days. Why? He feels neglected because she didn't love him enough to get to the elevator in time to catch him.

And, curiously enough, quarreling is a very important way of establishing deep bonds. When you fight, your soul is exposed for what it really is. That's why some people won't do anything with you before the first fight — no business, no love making, nothing. They're suspicious of people who never fight. They wonder if that peaceful calm is just surface, and what might be underneath the surface.

We are well aware that there really are beautiful people who live in great harmony and *don't* fight. We have been fortunate enough to meet some of them, and they are always a pleasure to be around. If you are among them, we thank you!

P.S.
We invite you to send us notes regarding the lovers' quarrels you've survived or even just heard about. And please include lots of details — we won't demand to know if they're true or whose stories they are!
For every lovers' quarrel we use, we will send you a free copy of the next edition of "Lovers' Quarrels: The Other Side Of Romance". We'll also be happy to

LATER...

After they've been at the party for a while, Ellen says she wants to go home. This annoys Dick and he says "Later! We just got here!" When she asks again, he accuses her of being a party-pooper and again puts her off. After another hour, Ellen says: "I'm really tired, would you please take me home?" He says: "Let me just say my good-byes." At two a.m., that's what he's still doing — saying his good-byes. She finally says "I'm leaving," walks out, and gets in the car. Just as she's about to drive off, she sees him come out of the house. She's suddenly so mad, she tries to run him down — and almost succeeds. She stops the car two blocks down the street, shaking with fear and rage. "Are you out of your mind?" he asks when he finally gets in. She drives home without saying a word. The next day...

sell you some wonderful Lovers' Quarrels greeting cards. We call them "Cards For Making Up." They're greeting cards that we've designed (a packet of ten will cost you $6 plus $1.50 for postage and handling). We think they will help patch up a lot of fights and, in addition, provide some wonderful entertainment.

DIET

For a long time he was urging her to lose weight, but she never would. Then one day she says, "Starting tomorrow I'm going on a diet." "I've heard that before," says Nick. She: "This time I mean it." "You've been saying that for months, but meanwhile you go on eating junk." "Please don't point out the inconsistencies in my behavior. That doesn't help! Be supportive instead." "I'd be very supportive, Laurie, provided I saw, just for once, that you really meant what you were saying."

WRONG?

She: "Can't you ever admit you're wrong?" He: "What for? You never let me forget it." She: "I wouldn't have to remind you of it if you ever admitted it." He: "When you stop pointing it out to me, that's when I'll start admitting it."

Whether these cards will work for you is, of course, something you will have to experiment with *yourself!*

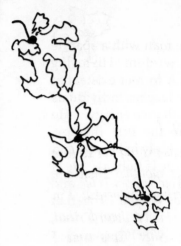

CANDIDATE

Frances is from a socially prominent family and Gary's running for Congress. They're scheduled to get married and her mother's planned a huge wedding. Then, suddenly, she has a panic attack and wonders if she isn't making a mistake. "I can't go through with this," she says, but her mother insists it's too late to call off the arrangements. Gary consoles her, saying "Feeling anxious is normal when you're getting married." What she hasn't told either him or her mother is that she's realized she doesn't love him. She feels she's about to sign her life away and she prays to God for help.

One thing we've discovered is that when you can tell others the stories of some of the lovers' quarrels you've lived through (without blame or anger but simply as entertainment) you'll start feeling a lot better about yourself and about your relationships.

So that's it, dear friends! For the moment, we have no more playful wisdom to impart to you. By all means *write to us* and share your quarrels with us — we promise not to tell a soul! Meanwhile, we hope you enjoy our little offering. God bless you! Our guess is that if you're at all like us, *you'll need it!*

William Ashoka Ross, PhD, is a gentle man with a sparkle in his eye—a man of few words and much wisdom. His loving encouragement has helped many people. A former existential and neo-Reichian psychotherapist, he now teaches individuals and groups how to integrate meditation with love energy. He believes that love and deep laughter are the best therapy. Trained in England, Dr. Ross has traveled widely in Europe and Asia and speaks many languages (his favorite is Italian). He is the author of *"Sex: There's More To It Than You've Been Told"* and *"Words From The Masters: A Guide To The God Within."* Together with Judy Ford, he has co-authored *"How To Find A Lover, Friend, or Companion."* He claims that the many lovers he has quarreled with have taught him more than any university. He lives in the Puget Sound area near Seattle.

Judy Ford, MSW, is a lively, enthusiastic parent whose motto is "never a dull moment." She is also a human relations consultant, a counselor in private practice, and a popular professional speaker. Judy's zest for living and her sparkle when she enters a room are immediately contagious — even when she is down. She loves to encounter people, to challenge them in a good-natured way, and to be challenged in turn. Judy has given talks to medical professionals, civic groups, and business organizations. The themes she likes to speak on include **Discovering Your Uniqueness**, a high energy romp in which Judy urges that your uniqueness is both fun and marketable, **Parenting,** in which Judy encourages parents to recognize their children's wisdom, **Courageous Living Following Loss**, and **Living With A Teenager**.

Playful Wisdom Press is the publishing branch of **Judy Ford & Company,** a company devoted to developing products and offering talks, workshops, and seminars that deal with love, relationships, healing, and playful wisdom.

How To Find A Lover, Friend or Companion is a book of encouragement! And it's written straight from the heart by Judy Ford, a wise and loving woman who cares passionately about life. It's full of fun, joy, and practical ideas for lovers of all ages, including what to say and where to say it. Because this book is so warm and caring, you'll feel as though you have a close personal friend by your side — counseling you, sharing with you, urging you on, telling you what pitfalls to avoid. A truly heart-warming book that will make you feel your life is chockfull of marvelous possibilities. "Wonderful, inspiring, enjoyable, and *very* helpful." *Many delightful illustrations!*

Sex: There's More To It Than You've Been Told is a wonderful book of insights about love and sex! "It has the effect of a gentle massage that eases away your tensions so that you can see sex as it could be in your life: relaxed, vital, renewing, a deep expression of a loving self." "A collection of clear, pithy and often witty observations." Talk show host: "Don't be dismayed at the seemingly small size of this little jewel; it's packed with thoughts, attitudes and information that can make a real difference." **The Chicago Tribune** calls it "a celebration of the healthful benefits of loving sexual relations." A nurse: "Makes you feel like celebrating and starting life all over again!" Therapist: *"A wonderful communication tool for couples!"*

How To Find A Lover, Friend... $4.95 plus $1 p.&h.

Sex: There's More To It... $4.95 plus $1 p.&h.

Send check or money order to:
Playful Wisdom Press, PO Box 834, Kirkland, WA 98083